16722

16722

The ILLUMINATED Declaration of Independence

Written by
THOMAS JEFFERSON

Penned in 1905 by
SHERMAN ELLSWORTH NOTESTINE

With an Introduction by
HENRY STEELE COMMAGER

HARMONY BOOKS
New York

S. E. NOTESTINE, PENMAN, HARRISBURG, PA.

Foreword

Publisher: BRUCE HARRIS
Editor: LINDA SUNSHINE
Assoc. Editor: NANCY CROW
Production: GENE CONNER, MURRAY SCHWARTZ
Book Design: KEN SANSONE
Cover Design: JIM DAVIS

Plates by Sherman Ellsworth Notestine are from the collection of John Blatteau and Paul Hirshorn.

The Introduction by Henry Steele Commager is reprinted by permission of G. P. Putnam's Sons from *Thomas Jefferson: The Man, His World, His Influence,* edited by Lally Weymouth (New York, 1974).

Unless otherwise noted, all illustrative photographs and woodcuts are used by courtesy of the Library of Congress.

Harmony Books, a division of Crown Publishers, Inc. 419 Park Avenue South, New York, New York 10016.

Published simultaneously in Canada by General Publishing Company Limited.
Printed in the United States of America.

LIBRARY OF CONGRESS
CATALOGING IN PUBLICATION DATA

Notestine, Sherman E   1865-1941.
    The illuminated Declaration of independence.

    1. United States. Declaration of independence.
I. United States. Declaration of independence. 1976.
II. Title.
E221.N67   1976   973.3′13   75-45218
ISBN 0-517-52544-5
ISBN 0-517-52545-3 pbk.

Sherman Ellsworth Notestine, the artist whose illuminated copy of the Declaration of Independence in thirty-five plates is reproduced in this volume, ranks with the best amateur penmen in an age when amateur penmanship flourished. An accountant for forty-five years with the Pennsylvania Railroad, he lived his entire life in central Pennsylvania. He was born on March 21, 1865, in Clearfield, raised in Marysville, and educated at the Williamsport Commercial College. He married and settled in Harrisburg, where he developed his consuming interests—cabinetmaking and penmanship.

Notestine pursued cabinetmaking throughout his life with his characteristic craftsmanship and attention to detail. He built chests and bookcases for his family and friends, frequently on demand, but always without charge. He approached penmanship, a natural outgrowth of his accounting work, the same way. His first efforts, done in his late thirties, were of popular religious subjects, such as the Twenty-third Psalm and the Lord's Prayer. Encouraged by the results, Notestine began in 1905 to work on what became his major composition and the focus of his life for the next ten years—the Declaration of Independence. During his working hours Notestine required absolute silence and isolation. He would work at a large table in his study, requiring no tools more special than his brushes, a wooden obelisk to act as an easel, and a magnifying glass to aid in the execution of the finer details. As he progressed, his work habits gradually intensified until he was working five or six hours every night.

Notestine's deepening commitment to the work is revealed in the composition of the plates. Although he was able to exploit the decorative possibilities of the text from the start, the initial plates were relatively monochromatic with most of the words rendered in script. By the second half of the work, he had completely discontinued the use of script in favor of more elaborate letter styles and had intensified his use of color washes and gold leaf. The final plates not only display Notestine's mature artistic talent, but also indicate the power the work had come to exert over him in the care and attention he gave to the words themselves. In these later stages, Notestine seems to have been reluctant to finish the project which had opened to him a universe for self-expression.

In 1915, Notestine completed the thirty-five plates of his illuminated Declaration of Independence. He was then fifty years old. With this major work realized, he turned from penmanship and again took up cabinetmaking. Fifteen years later, after his retirement from the Pennsylvania Railroad, Notestine decided to summarize his feelings toward the Declaration of Independence set by making an introductory plate. In this plate, lost in the 1950's, he stressed the craftsmanship and originality of the designs and claimed that the work was "the largest known pen specimen in the world."

In his later years, Notestine did make some attempts to sell the Declaration of Independence plates but decided against parting with the set. The drawings were never exhibited publicly during Notestine's lifetime. He died on August 22, 1941, in Harrisburg at the age of seventy-six.

—JOHN BLATTEAU and PAUL HIRSHORN

Introduction

BY HENRY STEELE COMMAGER

On 26 May 1776, that indefatigable correspondent John Adams, who represented Massachusetts at the Second Continental Congress, wrote exultantly to his friend James Warren that "every post and every day rolls in upon us independence like a torrent." Well might he rejoice, for this was what he and his cousin Samuel and his new friend Thomas Jefferson had hoped and worked for almost since the Congress had convened in May of the previous year, this rallying of public opinion to the cause of independence. It helped, to be sure, that the fatuous George III had proclaimed the colonies in rebellion, and thus helped the Americans to take him at his word. But the turning point, certainly in public opinion, had come with the publication, in January, 1776, of the sensational *Common Sense,* from the pen of Thomas Paine, the most gifted political propagandist in all history. And as if to vindicate Paine's aphorism that it was ridiculous for a continent to belong to an island, Washington proceeded to drive General Howe out of Boston, thus demonstrating that Americans need not stand on the defensive, but could vindicate themselves in military strategy quite as well as in political.

All that spring the political current flowed toward independence. In February the Congress had taken the ominous step of authorizing privateers; in March it ventured into diplomatic independence by sending the hapless Silas Deane to France to negotiate for aid; in April it declared economic independence by opening its ports to the trade of all nations —except Britain. No less impetuous was the radical change of sentiment in the states. As early as 26 March, South Carolina adopted a constitution which by implication repudiated the royal connection. Early the next month her sister state to the north instructed her delegates to the Congress to support independence, and in May, Rhode Island followed suit. Now Massachusetts and Virginia, from the beginning the leaders in organizing resistance to Britain, took action that proved decisive. On 10 May the Provisional Congress of Massachusetts voted to sound out the towns on the question of independence, and the towns declared that they were ready. Virginia did not lag behind. On 15 May a convention met at the historic Raleigh Tavern in Williamsburg and voted unanimously to call upon Congress to declare for independence. On the very day of the Virginia resolution, the Congress took the fateful step of voting that "every kind of authority under the Crown should be totally suppressed," and recommended that the states set up independent governments.

Now the stage was set for the historic event. On 7 June, Richard Henry Lee of Virginia—"the Cicero of America" —introduced three resolutions calling for independence, foreign alliances, and confederation. The radicals wanted unanimity, and voted to postpone the final vote for three weeks, thus allowing time for debate, and for the hesitant and the fainthearted to come over—or step out. Meantime Congress appointed a committee to prepare "a declaration of independence": Dr. Franklin, John Adams, Roger Sherman, Robert Livingstone, and, the youngest of all, Thomas Jefferson.

Jefferson had come up to the Continental Congress the previous year bringing with him "a reputation for literature, science and a happy talent of composition." His writings, said John Adams, who rarely had any good to say of others, "were remarkable for the peculiar felicity of expression." Back to Virginia in December, 1775, Jefferson had not found it possible to return to the Congress until mid-May of the next spring, just in time to achieve immortality. In part because of that "peculiar felicity of expression," in part because he had already had a reputation of working with dispatch, in part because it was thought that Virginia, as the oldest, the largest, and the most deeply committed of the states should take the lead, the committee unanimously turned to Jefferson to prepare a draft declaration. We know a good deal about the composition of that draft: that Jefferson wrote it standing up at his desk (still preserved) in the second-floor parlor of a young German bricklayer named Graff and that he completed it in two weeks. We have his word for it (which is not quite the same as knowing) that he "turned neither to book nor pamphlet" and that all the authority of the Declaration "rests on the harmonizing sentiments of the day, whether expressed in conversation, in letters, printed essays, or in the elementary books of public right, as Aristotle, Cicero, Locke, Sidney, etc." We know, too, that the body of the Declaration—that long and depressing catalog of the train of abuses and usurpations "designed to reduce the American people under absolute despotism"—was taken over from a parallel list of grievances which Jefferson had included in his draft constitution for Virginia only a few weeks earlier. And we can readily accept Jefferson's statement made fifty years later that the object of the Declaration was "an appeal to the tribunal of the world"—that "decent respect to the opinion of Mankind" invoked in the Declaration itself; certainly it was

> not to find out new principles, or new arguments, never before thought of; not merely to say things which had never been said before; but to place before mankind the common sense of the subject, in terms so plain and firm as to command their assent, and to justify ourselves in the independent stand we are compelled to take. Neither aiming at originality of principle or sentiment, nor yet copied from any particular and previous writing, it was intended to be an expression of the American mind, and to give to that expression the proper tone and spirit called for by the occasion.

In the end the Declaration was adopted pretty much as Jefferson had written it. There were, to be sure, a good many verbal changes—some twenty altogether (mostly improvements)—and Jefferson was persuaded to add three short paragraphs to his original text. The most grievous change, in his eyes, was the elimination of what John Adams called his "vehement philippic" against Negro slavery and the slave trade—one of the earliest expressions of Jefferson's lifelong detestation of the "peculiar institution." In some ways it was well that that paragraph dropped out, for in a curious way it struck a false note: it was rhetorical without being passionate, and it was bad history. Alas, these were not the reasons why it was eliminated, it was rather the reluctance of southern delegates to endorse so extreme an attack upon slavery.

After almost three days of debate Congress adopted the Declaration of Independence, though New York still refrained from voting. Jefferson remembered later that on the fourth of July "the Declaration was signed by every member present except Mr. Dickinson," and that legend has entered American history and art: witness the famous John Trumbull painting now hanging in the Library of Congress. Actually, however, it was not until 19 July that Congress provided that the Declaration be engrossed on parchment, and it was on 2 August that the document, "being engrossed and compared at the table" with Jefferson's original, was signed by all the members present.

Interestingly enough it is not Jefferson, but the more passionate and volatile John Adams, who has left us the most moving commentary on the events of this week when the Declaration was proposed, debated, and voted:

> You will think me transported with enthusiasm [he wrote to his wife Abigail], but I am not. I am well aware of the toil and blood, and treasure that it will cost us to maintain this declaration and support and defend these states. Yet through all the gloom I can see the rays of ravishing light and glory. I can see that the end is more than worth all the means, and that posterity will triumph in that day's transaction, even although we should rue it, which I trust in God we shall not.

When Jefferson wrote that the Declaration was "an expression of the American mind," what he referred to was almost certainly the Preamble. That Preamble was an expression of more than the American mind; it was an expression of the mind of the Enlightenment—of the Age of Reason. It was because Jefferson was so broadly cosmopolitan that he could sum up the thinking of the Enlightenment in the realm of political philosophy, and because he was so authentically American that he could transform that philosophy into American principles and realize it in American institutions.

Nothing is more fascinating than this Preamble, which summed up with matchless lucidity, logic, and eloquence the philosophy which presided over the argument for the Revolution, for the creation of a new political system, and for the vindication of the rights of man—and all in less than two hundred words! It is here that we find the expression of what is universal rather than parochial, what is permanent rather than transient, in the American Revolution. For where most of the body of the Declaration was retrospective, the Preamble was prospective: in the years to come it would be translated into the basic institutions of the American Republic, and not of the American alone.

Consider the opening words of the Declaration: "When, in the course of human events . . ." That places the Declaration, and the Revolution, at once in the appropriate setting, against the background not merely of American or of British but of universal history; that connects it with the experience of men everywhere, not at a moment of history, but in every era. This concept of the place of America in history is underlined by successive phrases of that great opening sentence. Thus the new nation is to assume its place "among the powers of the earth"; it is not the laws of the British Empire, or even of history, but of "Nature and Nature's God" which entitle Americans to an equal station; and it is "a decent respect to the opinions of *mankind*" that requires this justification. No other political document of the eighteenth century proclaimed so broad a purpose; no political document of our own day associates the United States so boldly with universal history and the cosmic system.

Turn then to those principles which Jefferson, serenely confident of their ultimate vindication, called "self-evident truths." Let us list them in order:

That all men are created equal;

That they are endowed with "unalienable rights";

That these rights include life, liberty, and the pursuit of happiness;

That it is to *secure* these rights that government is instituted among men;

That governments so instituted derive their powers from the consent of the governed;

That when a form of government becomes destructive of these ends, men may alter or abolish it; and

That men have the right, then, to institute new governments designed to effect their safety and happiness.

Now neither Jefferson nor the American people invented these principles. They were drawn from classical literature (with which all educated men of that day were familiar); they were elaborated by the generation of Lilburne, Cromwell, Sidney, Milton, and above all John Locke in seventeenth-century England; they were an integral part of the assumptions of the Age of Reason; they were—or appeared to be—rooted in American colonial experience. Jefferson's "self-evident truths" were no more original than were the arguments of Tom Paine's *Common Sense*; the Declaration of Independence was itself simply the common sense of the matter. That is one reason why it was so readily and so generally accepted; that was why it was read with rapture in so many parts of the globe. For the Declaration inspired radicals such as Joseph Priestley, and Horne Tooke, and John Cartwright in England, and rebels like Grattan and Fitzgerald in Ireland; it inspired the enthusiasm of those *philosophes* who were the precursors of the French Revolution, such as Mirabeau, Condorcet, Brissot, and Lafayette; it gave comfort to liberals everywhere: Johann Moser and Christoph Ebeling in Germany, Vittorio Alfieri and Gianrinaldi Carli in Italy, the intrepid Francis van der Kemp in Holland, who found refuge in America, Henrik Steffens in Denmark, and Isaak Iselin in Basel. It fired the spirit of Francisco Miranda, and of many other leaders of the South American crusade for independence, and perhaps freedom. It entered into the mainstream of history, and worked like a ferment all through the nineteenth and twentieth centuries; in 1945 Ho Chi Minh proclaimed the independence of Vietnam with a declaration modeled on that which Thomas Jefferson had written 170 years earlier.

What Americans did was more important than invent new principles; in the telling phrase of John Adams "they *realized* the theories of the wisest writers." They actualized them, they legalized them, they institutionalized them. That was, and remains, the supreme achievement of the American Revolution; indeed, in the longer perspective, that *was* the American Revolution.

Thus—if we take up Jefferson's principles one by one—the idea of natural rights was as old as Greek philosophy and one which had been invoked again and again over the centuries. But it was only then, for the first time, that it was formalized and written into constitutional guarantees, only then that the notion which had for so long lingered in the realm of the abstract was endowed with life and clothed in the majestic raiment of the law. Thus for over two thousand years philosophers had argued that government is limited; the revolutionary generation went further, and insisted that God himself was bound by his own laws of justice and mercy. All well enough as long as men gave only lip service to this revolutionary idea. For in fact no government ever had been really limited, not voluntarily anyway: the history of government (as Americans read it) had been an unbroken record of tyranny, and every monarch in Europe still exercised tyranny: even George III, particularly George III. When Jefferson wrote that it was "to preserve rights" that governments were instituted among men, he meant just what he said, and so did those who signed the Declaration: that the function of government was to preserve the inalienable rights of men, and that if government failed in this duty, it forfeited its claim to legitimacy. After all, even before he wrote the Declaration, Jefferson had drawn up a model constitution and bill of rights for Virginia (neither was adopted but some of his suggestions were incorporated into both), and both these documents were designed to limit the power of government with the utmost care. Soon constitution-makers were busy in every state of the new nation doing what Jefferson and his associates had done so well in the oldest of American commonwealths.

So, too, with the principle that government is formed by compact, and that governments thus formed derive all their power from that compact and are limited by its terms. An old theory, this, one which had bemused philosophers for centuries and had received classic formulation by John Locke in the seventeenth and Jean Jacques Rousseau in the eighteenth centuries. Whether in some remote past men ever had come together to set up government, we do not know; what we do know is that this was the way government orig-inated in America, and the way it continued to originate for two centuries: in the compact in the hold of the tiny *May-flower*; in those Fundamental Orders which the freemen of three frontier towns along the Connecticut drew up in 1639; in the constitution formed by the pioneers of the short-lived Transylvania colony in 1775; by the settlers of early Oregon who in 1843 convened the so-called Wolf conven-tions, took affairs into their own hands, and drew up the first Organic Law west of the Rockies; by the followers of John Frémont, who in 1846 launched the Bear Flag revolt, and met together to set up a "Republican Government which shall ensure . . . liberty and virtue."

Thus, too, with what now seems a kind of intuitive genius, Americans solved that most intractable problem: how men make government—they institutionalized the solution in the constitutional convention, a contrivance which has some claim to be the most important political institution of modern times, for it provided the basic mechanisms of democracy. And along with these, it provided a legal way for men to "alter or abolish" governments: to alter by amendments, or to abolish by wiping the slate clean and drawing up a wholly new constitution. Thus, for the first time in history, men legalized revolution. As Alexander Hamilton wrote, the Constitutional Convention "substituted the mild influence of the law for the violent and sanguinary agency of the sword." Jefferson put it more elaborately: "Happy for us that when we find our constitution defective and insufficient to secure the happiness of our people, we can assemble with all the coolness of philosophers and set it to rights, while every other nation on earth must have recourse to arms to amend or restore their constitutions."

The implementation of other principles in the Preamble was more difficult if only because they did not lend them-selves so readily to institutionalization. What, after all, did Jefferson mean by such terms as "created equal" or "pursuit of happiness"? These are not only difficult questions, they are in a sense unfair questions. No language, as James Madison observed, "is so copious as to supply words and phrases for every complex idea or so correct as not to in-clude many equivocally denoting different ideas."

There is little doubt that Jefferson used, and that his asso-ciates in the Congress endorsed, the term "created equal" in a quite literal sense, for that is the sense in which the Enlightenment embraced and applied the term. What Jeffer-son meant was that in the eyes of nature (and doubtless of God) every child was *born* equal. All subsequent inequali-ties, those of race, color, sex, class, wealth, even of talents, derived not from nature but from society, or government, or law. Nature, after all, did not decree the inequality of blacks to whites. Nature did not decree the subordination of the female to the male—there was some ground for thinking it might be the other way around. Nature did not impose class distinctions, or political distinctions, or religious distinc-tions; it was not even certain that nature imposed physical or intellectual distinctions. Give every child an equal chance, from birth, at health, education, and happiness, and who

could foresee the result? This was not merely Jefferson's idea, but one widely held by the *philosophes,* whose perva-sive principle was that men were everywhere and at all times fundamentally the same. Yet neither the *philosophes* nor the enlightened despots of the Old World made any effort to translate this principle of equality into practice, as did the Americans, Jefferson among them. That they did not suc-ceed is a reflection on their authority, not on their wisdom. After all, we of the twentieth century have not succeeded either, yet we do have the authority. What we lack is the will.

"Pursuit of happiness" is a more elusive phrase, yet the idea that God and nature intended that men should be happy was a commonplace of eighteenth-century thought. In the Old World, however, happiness tended to be an elitist con-cept, something that the privileged few might possibly achieve by cultivating beauty and wisdom and leisure and the social graces: an expensive business, this, and not ordi-narily available to the masses of the people. As America had no elite—not, certainly, in the Old World sense of the term —happiness here was presumed to be available to all who were white, and it consisted, not in the enjoyment of art and literature, science and philosophy, and social position, but rather in material comfort, freedom, independence, and access to opportunity. Happiness meant milk for the chil-dren and meat on the table, a well-built house and a well-filled barn, freedom from the tyranny of the state, the superstition of the church, the authority of the military, and the malaise of ignorance. Jefferson, who knew and indulged himself in the Old World forms of happiness, was entirely willing to abandon them—and indeed to banish them from his own country—in favor of the more simple, the more innocent, and the more just happiness which he thought available in his own country. And to the attainment of these, and their preservation, he made not only philosophical con-tributions but practical contributions as important and as far-reaching as those made by any other man of his time.

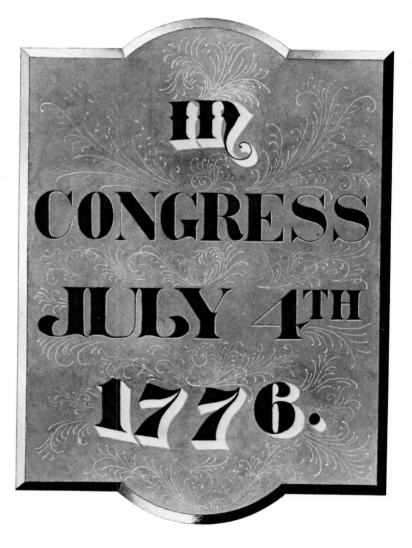

IN CONGRESS JULY 4TH 1776.

The original and official copy on parchment of the Declaration of Independence, now housed in the National Archives, Washington, D.C.

THE

UNANIMOUS

DECLARATION

OF

THE

THIRTEEN

United States

OF

AMERICA

When in the course of human events it becomes necessary for one people to dissolve the political bands which have connected them with another, and to assume among the powers of the earth the separate and equal station to which the Laws of Nature and of Nature's God entitles* them, a decent respect to the opinions of mankind requires that they should declare the causes which impel them to the separation.

---

*Notestine's mistake. "Entitle" is of course correct and is so used in the original copy of the Declaration.

On June 7, 1776, Richard Henry Lee of Virginia (*right*) presented his Resolution to the Continental Congress: "That these United Colonies are, and of right, ought to be, free and independent states . . ." The document shown here is believed to be in Lee's own hand.

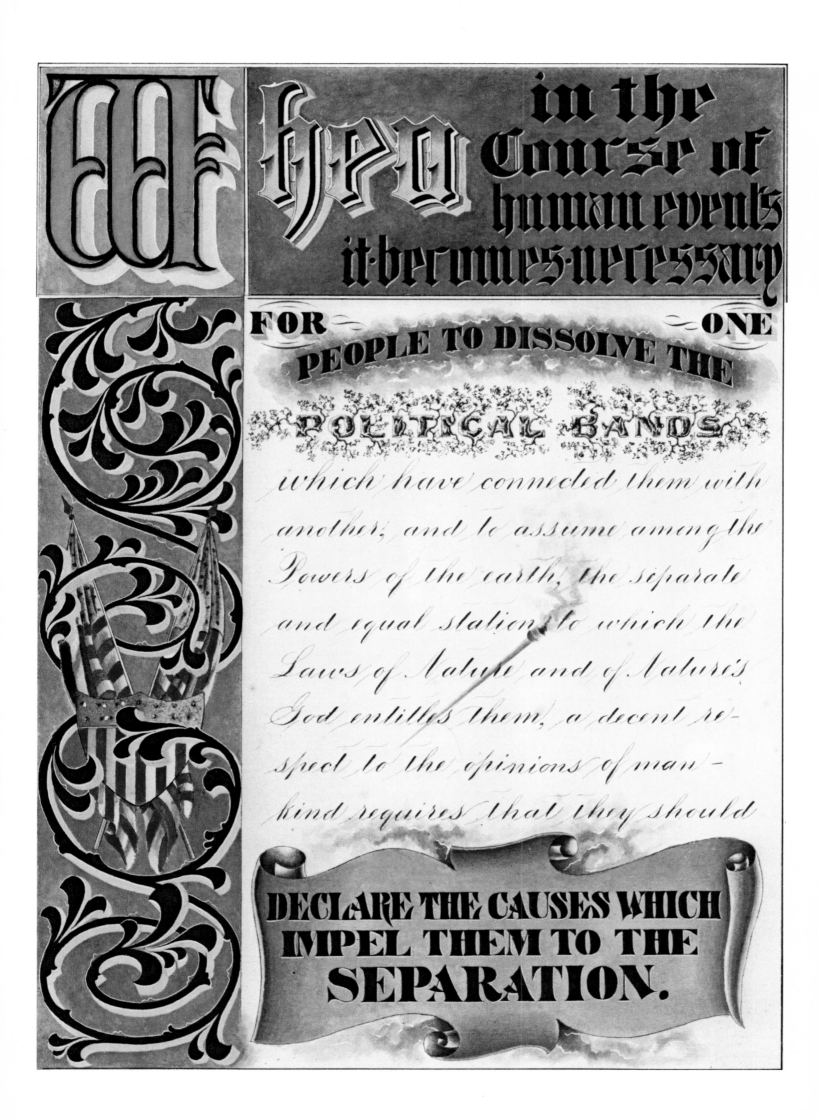

We hold these truths to be self-evident: that all men are created equal, that they are endowed by their creator with certain unalienable rights, that among these are Life, Liberty and the pursuit of Happiness. That to secure these rights Governments are instituted among Men, deriving their just powers from the consent of the governed. That whenever any Form of Government becomes destructive of these ends, it is . . .

Thomas Jefferson wrote the Declaration of Independence on this portable desk which he had designed himself. The engraving of Jefferson is from a painting by Charles Willson Peale, 1791.

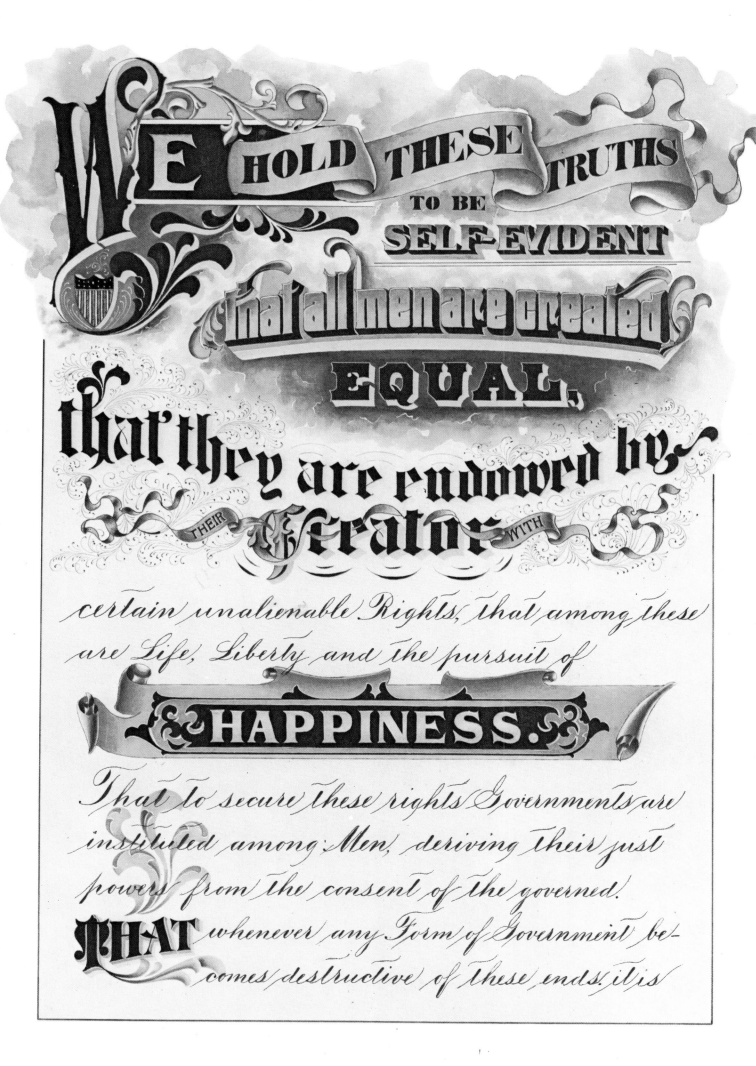

WE HOLD THESE TRUTHS TO BE SELF-EVIDENT

that all men are created EQUAL, that they are endowed by THEIR Creator WITH certain unalienable Rights, that among these are Life, Liberty and the pursuit of

HAPPINESS.

That to secure these rights Governments are instituted among Men, deriving their just powers from the consent of the governed! THAT whenever any Form of Government becomes destructive of these ends, it is

... the Right of the People to alter or to abolish it and to institute new Government, laying its foundation on such principles and organizing its powers in such form, as to them shall seem most likely to effect their Safety and Happiness.

As a result of the Boston Tea Party, the British closed the port of Boston. According to a contemporary London cartoon, the Bostonians got what they deserved for having climbed on the Liberty Tree in the first place. Colonists who were guilty of capital crimes against England would be caged and left to starve. The gift of fish to the prisoners presumably alludes to codfish sent to Marblehead, one of the many gifts to the distressed port.

Prudence, indeed, will dictate that governments long established should not be changed for light and transient causes; and, accordingly, all experience hath shown that mankind are more disposed to suffer, while evils are sufferable, than to right themselves by abolishing the forms to which they have been accustomed.* But when a long train of ...

* Notestine's mistake. "Are accustomed" is the correct wording.

The first page of Thomas Jefferson's original four-page draft of the Declaration of Independence.

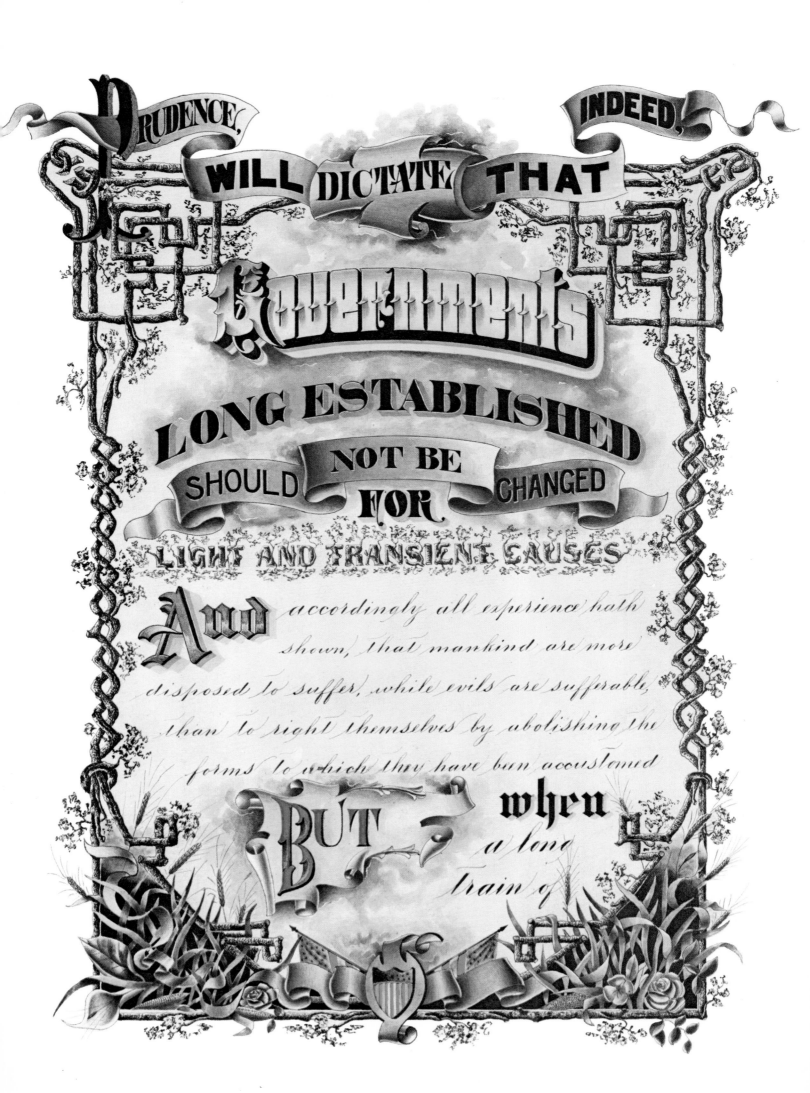

...Abuses and Usurpations, pursuing invariably the same object, evinces a design to reduce them under Absolute Despotism, it is their right, it is their duty, to throw off such Government and to provide new Guards for their future security. Such has been the patient sufferance of these Colonies...

Paul Revere's engraving of a British cartoon depicting the presence of martial law and the administration of the tea tax after the Boston Tea Party, originally published in the *London Magazine*, April, 1774. The English saw their colonies as a wild maiden who needed a little doctoring. Revere agreed entirely that the doctoring would help produce a cure—complete rebellion against King George. Britannia in the background shields her eyes from the sight—a touch Revere may have added to the original British version.

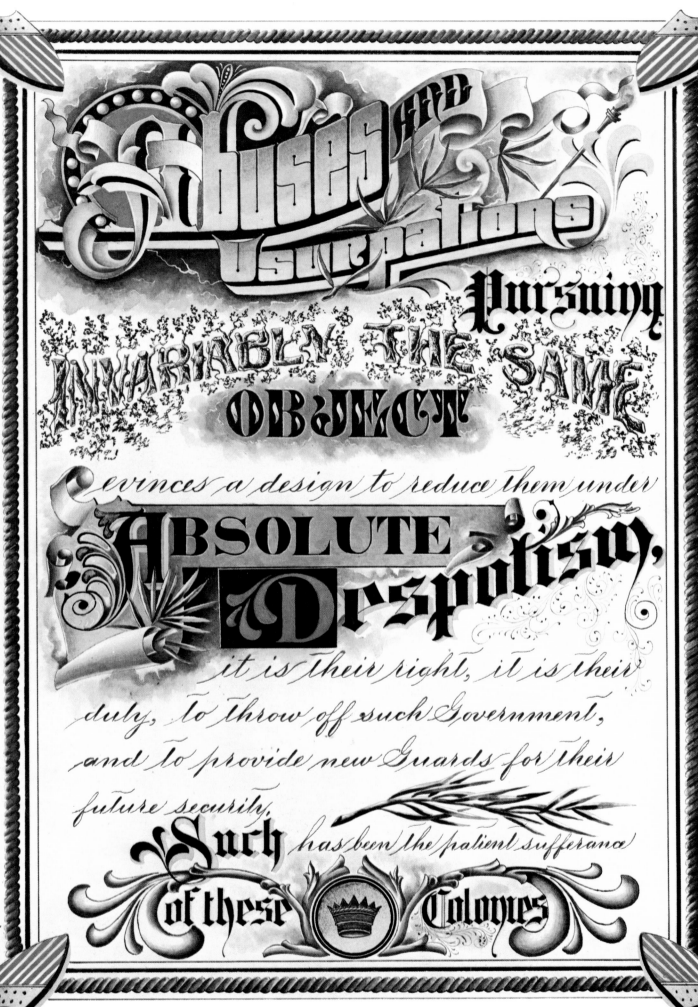

. . . and such is now the necessity which constrains them to alter their former Systems of Government. The history of the present King of Great Britain is a history of repeated injuries and usurpations, all having in direct object the establishment of an absolute tyranny over these States.

Maxfield Parrish's satiric rendition of the presentation of the colonists' grievances to King George III, painted for *Collier's Magazine* in 1901.

and such IS NOW THE **necessity** which constrains them to alter their former Systems of GOVERNMENT. The history of the present King of Great Britain is a history of repeated injuries and usurpations, all having in direct object the establishment of an absolute TYRANNY over these States.

To prove this, let facts be submitted to a candid world. He has refused his Assent to Laws, the most wholesome and necessary for the public good. He has forbidden his Governors to pass Laws of immediate and pressing importance, unless suspended in their operation till his Assent should be obtained; and when so suspended, he has utterly neglected to attend to them. He has refused to pass other Laws for the accommodation of large districts of people, unless those people would ...

Drafting the Declaration of Independence. The Committee—Benjamin Franklin, Thomas Jefferson, John Adams, Robert Livingston and Roger Sherman. Engraved from an original painting by Channel and published in 1861 by Johnson Fry & Co., New York.

To prove this, let Facts be submitted to a candid World.

He has refused his Assent to Laws, the most wholesome and necessary for the public good.

He has forbidden his Governors to pass Laws of immediate and pressing importance, unless suspended in their operation till his Assent should be obtained; and when so suspended, he has utterly neglected to attend to them.

He has refused to pass other Laws for the accommodation of large districts of people, unless those People would

S. E. NOTESTINE, PENMAN HARRISBURG

...relinquish the right of Representation in the Legislature, a right inestimable to them and formidable to tyrants only. He has called together legislative bodies at places unusual, uncomfortable, and distant from the depository of their Public Records, for the sole purpose of fatiguing them into compliance with ...

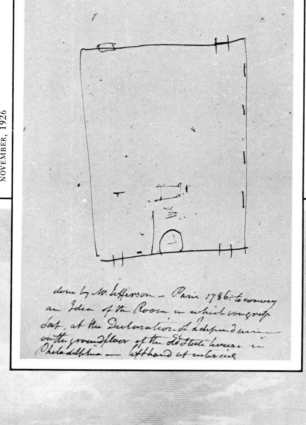

Below: An engraving of the State House in Philadelphia where the Declaration of Independence was adopted on July 4, 1776. *Left:* A sketch to which the painter John Trumbull added the note: "done by Mr. Jefferson—Paris, 1786—to convey an Idea of the Room in which Congress sat at the Declaration of Independence on the ground floor of the old state house in Philadelphia."

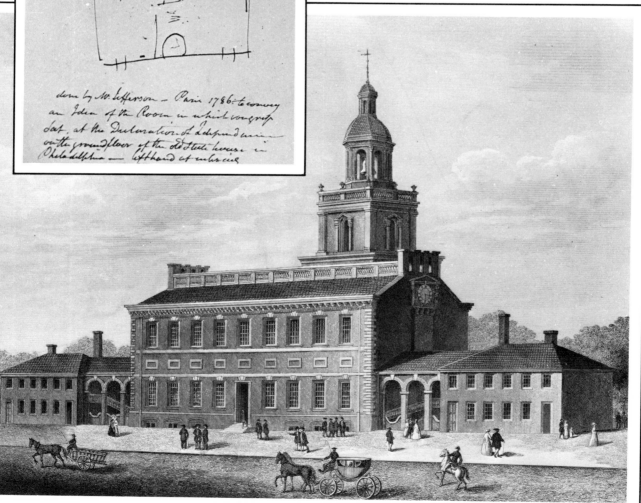

RELINQUISH

THE RIGHT

OF

REPRESENTATION

in the

LEGISLATURE.

A right inestimable to them

and **FORMIDABLE** to

TYRANTS ONLY.

He has called together legislative bodies at places unusual, uncomfortable, and distant from the depository of their Public Records, for the sole purpose of fatiguing them

INTO *compliance* WITH

S. E. NOTESTINE, PENMAN HARRISBURG, PA.

...his measures. He has dissolved Representative Houses repeatedly for opposing with manly firmness his invasion* on the rights of the people. He has refused, for a long time after such dissolutions, to cause others to be elected; whereby the Legislative Powers, incapable of annihilation, have returned to the People at large for their exercise; the State remaining in the meantime exposed ...

*"Invasions" is correct.

The second page of Thomas Jefferson's original draft of the Declaration of Independence.

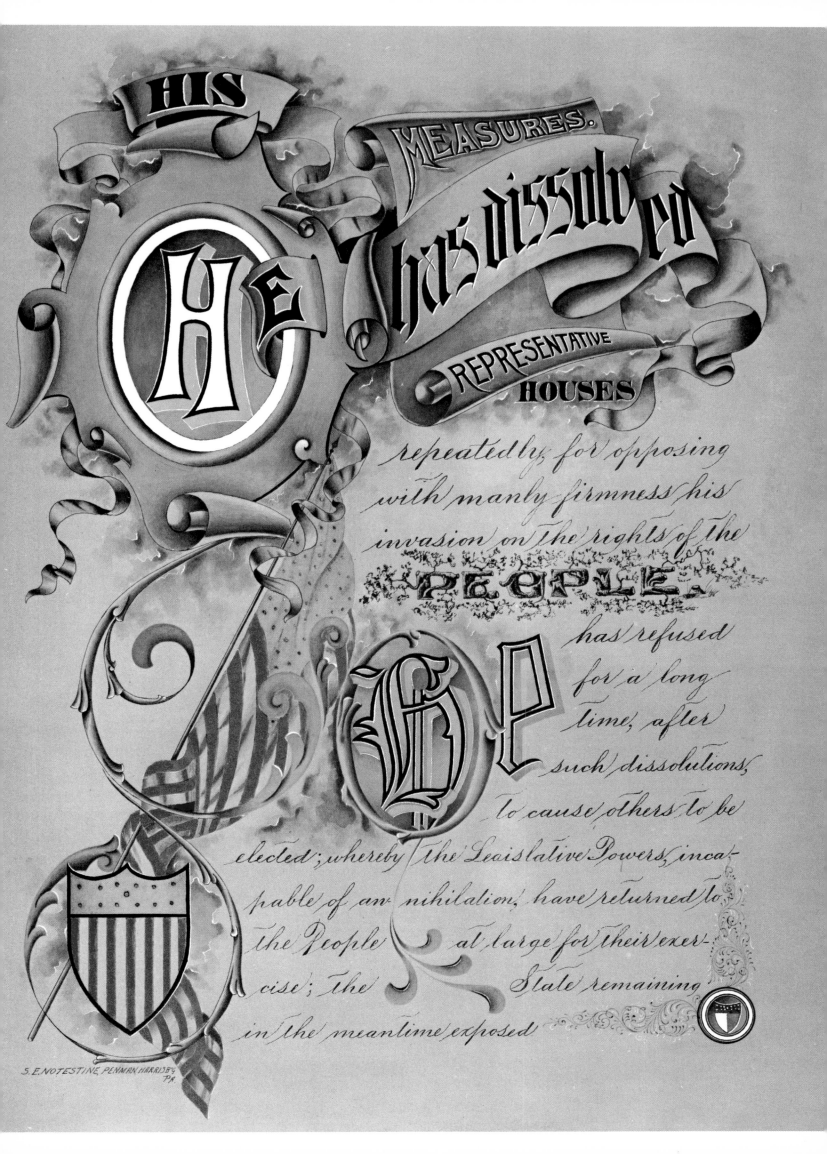

HIS MEASURES.

He has dissolved REPRESENTATIVE HOUSES

repeatedly, for opposing with manly firmness, his invasion on the rights of the PEOPLE.

He has refused for a long time, after such dissolutions, to cause others to be elected; whereby the Legislative Powers, incapable of annihilation, have returned to the People at large for their exercise; the State remaining in the meantime exposed

S.E. NOTESTINE, PENMAN HARRISBG PA

...to all the dangers of invasion from without and convulsions within. He has endeavoured to prevent the population of these States; for that purpose obstructing the Laws for Naturalization of Foreigners, refusing to pass others to encourage their migration hither, and raising the conditions of new Appropriations of Lands. He has obstructed the ...

Howard Pyle's conception of the reading of the Declaration of Independence before Washington's army, New York, July 9, 1776.

TO ALL

THE DANGERS OF INVASION

from

WITHOUT, and CONVULSIONS WITHIN.

He Has endeavoured to prevent the population of these

STATES

for that purpose obstructing the Laws for Naturalization of Foreigners; refusing to pass others to encourage their migration hither, and raising the conditions of new Appropriations of Lands.

has obstructed the

...administration of Justice, by refusing his Assent to Laws for establishing Judiciary Powers. He has made Judges dependent on his Will alone, for the tenure of their offices, and the amount and payment of their salaries. He has erected a multitude of New Offices,...

Signers of the Declaration of Independence

Delegate and State	Vocation	Birthplace	Born			Died		
Adams, John (Mass.)	Lawyer	Braintree (Quincy), Mass	1735,	Oct.	30	1826,	July	4
Adams, Samuel (Mass.)	Political Leader	Boston, Mass.	1722,	Sept.	27	1803,	Oct.	2
Bartlett, Josiah (N. H.)	Physician, Jurist	Amesbury, Mass.	1729,	Nov.	21	1795,	May	19
Braxton, Carter (Va.)	Farmer	King & Queen C.H. Va.	1736,	Sept.	10	1797,	Oct.	10
Carroll, Chas. of Carrollton (Md.)	Lawyer	Annapolis, Md.	1737,	Sept.	19	1832,	Nov.	14
Chase, Samuel (Md.)	Jurist	Princess Anne, Md.	1741,	April	17	1811,	June	19
Clark, Abraham (N. J.)	Surveyor	Elizabeth, N. J.	1726,	Feb.	15	1794,	Sept.	15
Clymer, George (Pa.)	Merchant	Philadelphia, Pa.	1739,	March	16	1813,	Jan.	23
Ellery, William (R. I.)	Jurist	Newport, R. I.	1727,	Dec.	22	1820,	Feb.	15
Floyd, William (N. Y.)	Soldier	Brookhaven, N. Y.	1734,	Dec.	17	1821,	Aug.	4
Franklin, Benjamin (Pa.)	Printer, Publisher	Boston, Mass.	1706,	Jan.	17	1790,	April	17
Gerry, Elbridge (Mass.)	Merchant	Marblehead, Mass.	1744,	July	17	1814,	Nov.	23
Gwinnett, Button (Ga.)	Merchant	Down Hatherly, Eng.	1732			1777,	May	19
Hall, Lyman (Ga.)	Physician	Wallingford, Conn.	1724,	April	12	1790,	Oct.	19
Hancock, John (Mass.)	Merchant	Braintree (Quincy), Mass.	1737,	Jan.	12	1793,	Oct.	8
Harrison, Benjamin (Va.)	Farmer	Berkeley, Va.	1726,	April	5	1791,	April	24
Hart, John (N. J.)	Farmer	Stonington, Conn.	(1707-1711?)			1779,	May	11
Hewes, Joseph (N. C.)	Merchant	Kingston, N. J.	1730,	Jan.	23	1779,	Nov.	10
Heyward, Thos. Jr. (S. C.)	Lawyer, Farmer	St. Luke's Parish, S. C.	1746,	July	28	1809,	March	6
Hooper, William (N. C.)	Lawyer	Boston, Mass.	1742,	June	28	1790,	Oct.	14
Hopkins, Stephen (R. I.)	Jurist, Educator	Providence, R. I.	1707,	March	7	1785,	July	13
Hopkinson, Francis (N. J.)	Jurist, Author	Philadelphia, Pa.	1737,	Sept.	21	1791,	May	9
Huntington, Samuel (Conn.)	Jurist	Windham County, Conn.	1731,	July	3	1796,	Jan.	5
Jefferson, Thomas (Va.)	Lawyer	Old Shadwell, Va.	1743,	April	13	1826,	July	4
Lee, Richard Henry (Va.)	Farmer	Stratford, Va.	1732,	Jan.	20	1794,	June	19
Lee, Francis Lightfoot (Va.)	Farmer	Stratford, Va.	1734,	Oct.	14	1797,	Jan.	11
Lewis, Francis (N. Y.)	Merchant	Landaff, Wales	1713,	March		1803,	Dec.	30
Livingston, Philip (N. Y.)	Merchant	Albany, N. Y.	1716,	Jan.	15	1778,	June	12
Lynch, Thomas Jr. (S. C.)	Farmer	Winyah, S. C.	1749,	Aug.	5	1779,	(at sea)	
McKean, Thomas (Del.)	Lawyer	New London, Pa.	1734,	March	19	1817,	June	24
Middleton, Arthur (S. C.)	Farmer	Charleston, S. C.	1742,	June	26	1787,	Jan.	1
Morris, Lewis (N. Y.)	Farmer	Morrisania, N. Y. (N.Y.C.)	1726,	April	8	1798,	Jan.	22
Morris, Robert (Pa.)	Merchant	Liverpool, Eng.	1734,	Jan.	20	1806,	May	8
Morton, John (Pa.)	Jurist	Ridley, Pa.	1724			1777,	April	
Nelson, Thos. Jr. (Va.)	Farmer	Yorktown, Va.	1738,	Dec.	26	1789,	Jan.	4
Paca, William (Md.)	Jurist	Abingdon, Md.	1740,	Oct.	31	1799,	Oct.	23
Paine, Robert Treat (Mass.)	Jurist	Boston, Mass.	1731,	March	11	1814,	May	12
Penn, John (N. C.)	Lawyer	Near Port Royal, Va.	1741,	May	17	1788,	Sept.	14
Read, George (Del.)	Jurist	Near North East, Md.	1733,	Sept.	18	1798,	Sept.	21
Rodney, Caesar (Del.)	Jurist	Dover, Del.	1728,	Oct.	7	1784,	June	29
Ross, George (Pa.)	Jurist	New Castle, Del.	1730,	May	10	1779,	July	14
Rush, Benjamin (Pa.)	Physician	Byberry, Pa. (Philadelphia)	1745,	Dec.	24	1813,	April	19
Rutledge, Edward (S. C.)	Lawyer	Charleston, S. C.	1749,	Nov.	23	1800,	Jan.	23
Sherman, Roger (Conn.)	Lawyer	Newton, Mass.	1721	April	19	1793,	July	23
Smith, James (Pa.)	Lawyer	Dublin, Ireland	1713			1806,	July	11
Stockton, Richard (N. J.)	Lawyer	Near Princeton, N. J.	1730,	Oct.	1	1781,	Feb.	28
Stone, Thomas (Md.)	Lawyer	Charles County, Md.	1743			1787,	Oct.	5
Taylor, George (Pa.)	Ironmaster	Ireland	1716			1781,	Feb.	23
Thornton, Matthew (N. H.)	Physician	Ireland	1714			1803,	June	24
Walton, George (Ga.)	Jurist	Prince Edward County, Va.	1741			1804,	Feb.	2
Whipple, William (N. H.)	Merchant, Jurist	Kittery, Maine	1730,	Jan.	14	1785,	Nov.	28
Williams, William (Conn.)	Merchant	Lebanon, Conn.	1731,	April	23	1811,	Aug.	2
Wilson, James (Pa.)	Jurist	Carskerdo, Scotland	1742,	Sept.	14	1798,	Aug.	28
Witherspoon, John (N. J.)	Educator	Gifford, Scotland	1723,	Feb.	5	1794,	Nov.	15
Wolcott, Oliver (Conn.)	Jurist	Windsor, Conn.	1726,	Dec.	1	1797,	Dec.	1
Wythe, George (Va.)	Lawyer	Elizabeth City, Va.	1726			1806,	June	8

Of the fifty-six signers of the Declaration of Independence, exactly half were lawyers or jurists. One of the foremost lawyers was John Adams, depicted in an engraving made from an oil painting by Gilbert Stuart.

ADMINISTRATION of JUSTICE,

by refusing his Assent to Laws for establishing

JUDICIARY POWERS

HE has made Judges dependent on his Will alone, for the tenure of their offices, and the amount and payment of their salaries.

HE has erected a multitude of New Offices,

S.E. NOTESTINE, PENMAN, HARRISBURG PA

...and sent hither swarms of Officers to harass our People and eat out their substance. He has kept among us, in times of peace, Standing Armies without the Consent of our Legislature. He has affected to render the ...

An engraving of forty-nine of the fifty-six signers of the Declaration of Independence.

and

sent hither swarms of
Officers to harass our People,
and eat out their substance.

He has kept among
us, in times of peace,
Standing Ar-
mies without
the Consent of
our Legislature.

He has affected
to render the

...Military independent of and superior to the Civil Power. He has combined with others to subject us to a jurisdiction foreign to our constitution and unacknowledged by our laws;...

Paul Revere's famous engraving, "The Fruits of Arbitrary Power, or The Bloody Massacre," depicting a scene in Boston, 1770. This took place almost four years prior to the Boston Tea Party. Although two British soldiers were branded with hot irons on the hands as punishment for firing on the Bostonians, it was Revere's sentiment that eventually prevailed.

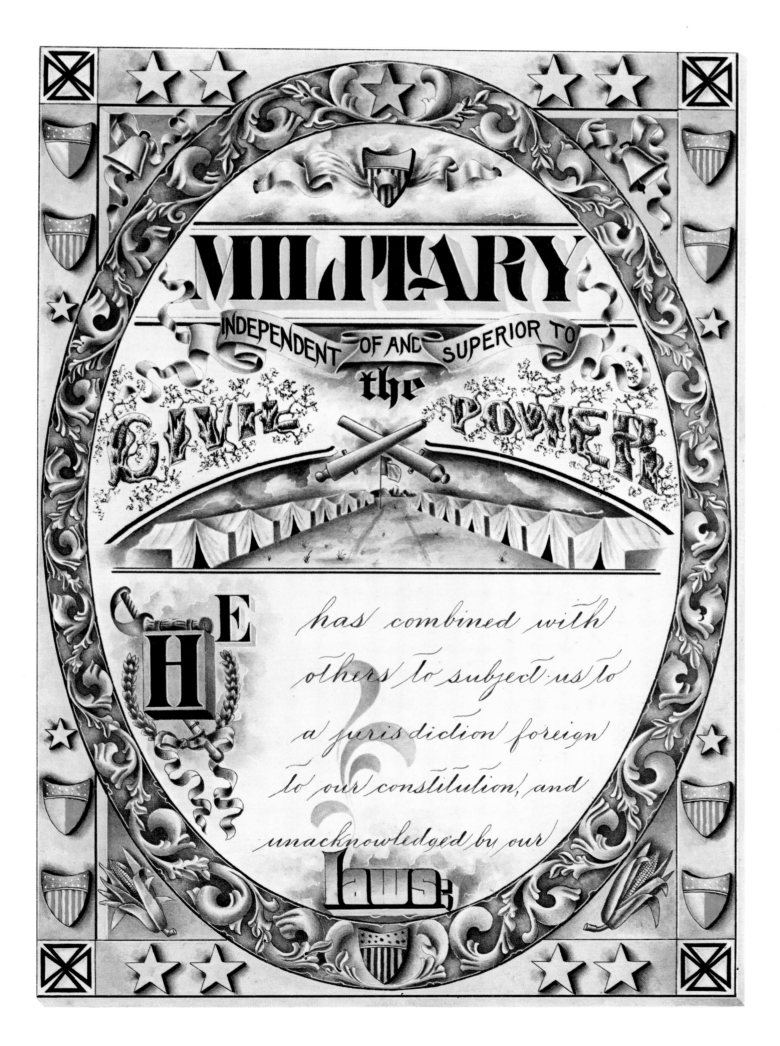

MILITARY

INDEPENDENT OF AND SUPERIOR TO the

CIVIL POWER

He has combined with others to subject us to a jurisdiction foreign to our constitution, and unacknowledged by our laws:

...giving his Assent to their acts of pretended Legislation: For quartering large bodies of armed troops among us: For protecting them, by a mock Trial, from Punishment for any...

A British official appointed to collect taxes in Boston is about to be tarred and feathered, January 20, 1775.

...murders which they should commit on
the inhabitants of these States: For cutting off our Trade
with all parts of the world:

"Fanning's Atrocity." An
example of the wanton murder
of American colonists.

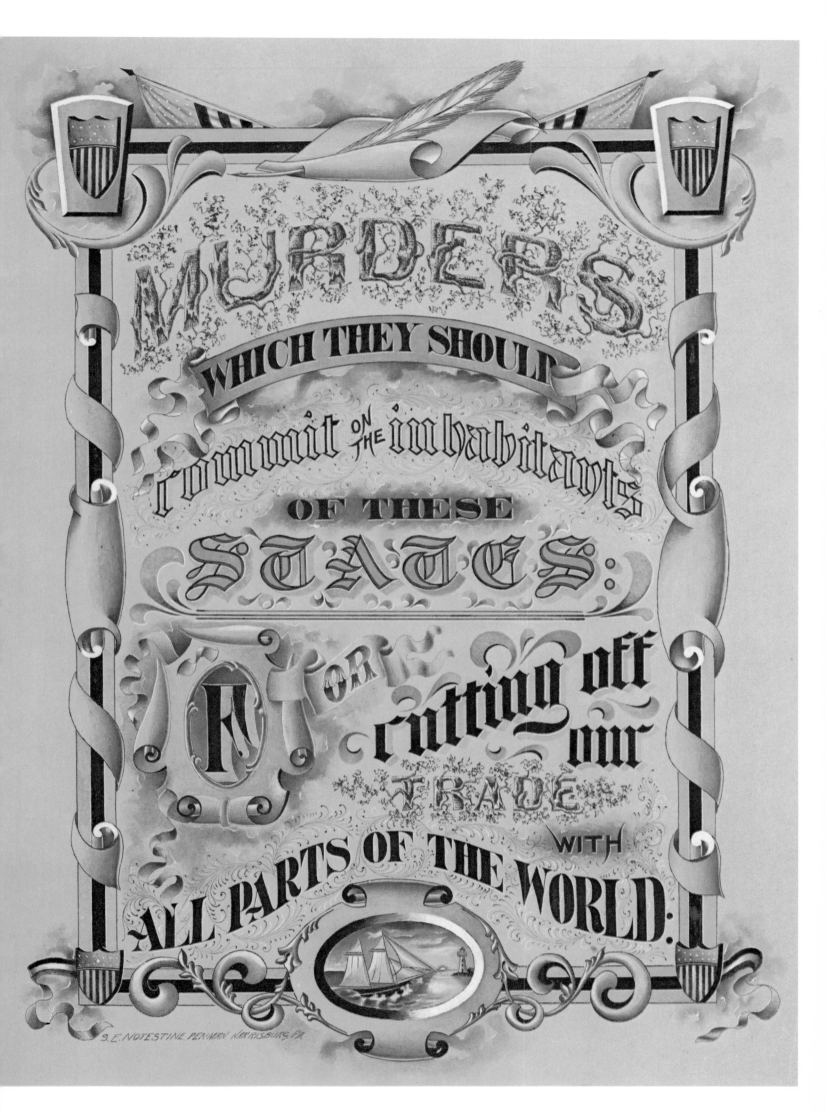

MURDERS WHICH THEY SHOULD commit on the inhabitants OF THESE STATES: OR cutting off our TRADE with ALL PARTS OF THE WORLD.

S. E. NOTESTINE, PENMAN, HARRISBURG, PA.

For imposing Taxes on us without our Consent: For depriving us in many cases of the benefits of Trial by Jury: For transporting us beyond Seas to be tried for pretended offenses:

Parade to protest the Stamp Act in New York. The banner reads "England's Folly & America's Ruin." Passed in 1765, the Stamp Act was the first direct tax imposed on the colonies.

For IMPOSING TAXES ON US without our Consent: For depriving us in many cases, of the benefits of TRIAL BY JURY For transporting us beyond Seas to be tried for PRETENDED OFFENSES.

S.E. NOTESTINE, PENMAN, HARRISBURG, PA

For abolishing the free System of English Laws in a neighbouring Province, establishing therein an Arbitrary government, and enlarging its Boundaries so as to render it at once an example and fit instrument for introducing the same absolute rule into these Colonies:

DRAWING BY EDWIN AUSTIN ABBEY

After hearing the Declaration of Independence for the first time, colonists in Philadelphia knocked down a wooden copy of the Royal Arms and burned it in the streets.

for abolishing

THE FREE

System of English

LAWS

in a neighbouring Province, establishing therein an Arbitrary government, and enlarging its Boundaries so as to render it at once an

EXAMPLE

and fit instrument for introducing the same absolute rule into these

COLONIES:

For taking away our Charters, abolishing our most valuable Laws, and altering fundamentally the forms of our Governments:

The third page of Thomas Jefferson's original draft of the Declaration of Independence.

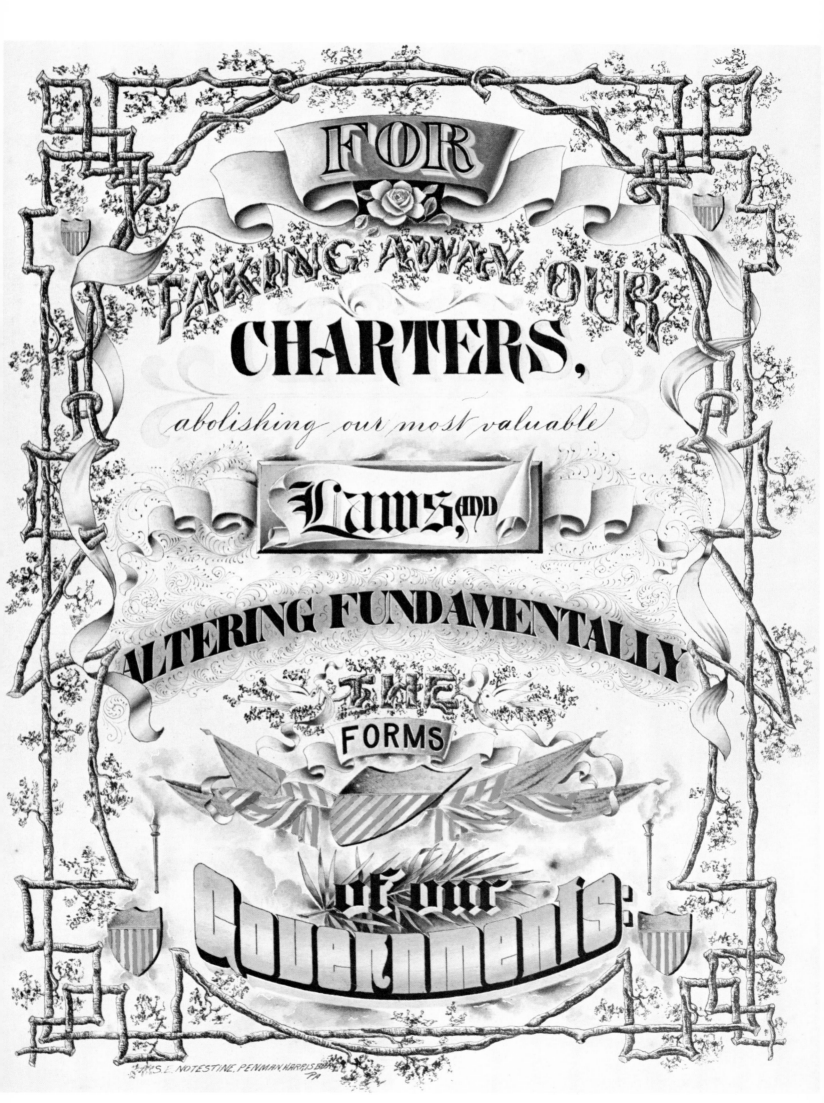

FOR

TAKING AWAY OUR

CHARTERS,

abolishing our most valuable

Laws, and

ALTERING FUNDAMENTALLY

THE

FORMS

of our

Governments:

For suspending our own Legislatures, and declaring themselves invested with power to legislate for us in all cases whatsoever. He has abdicated Government here, by declaring us out of his protection and waging war against us.

Robt. Morris.   Saml. Adams.   Benjamin Rush.   Charles Carroll   Rev. John Witherspoon.   John Adams   John Hancock   Edwd. Rutledge.
Richard Henry Lee

JOHN HANCOCK'S DEFIANCE.

JULY 4TH 1776.

The Declaration of Independence being fully adopted, John Hancock, President of the Continental Congress took up the pen and signed his name to it in a large bold hand; then rising he said, "There! John Bull can read my name without spectacles, and may double his reward for my head. That is my defiance!"

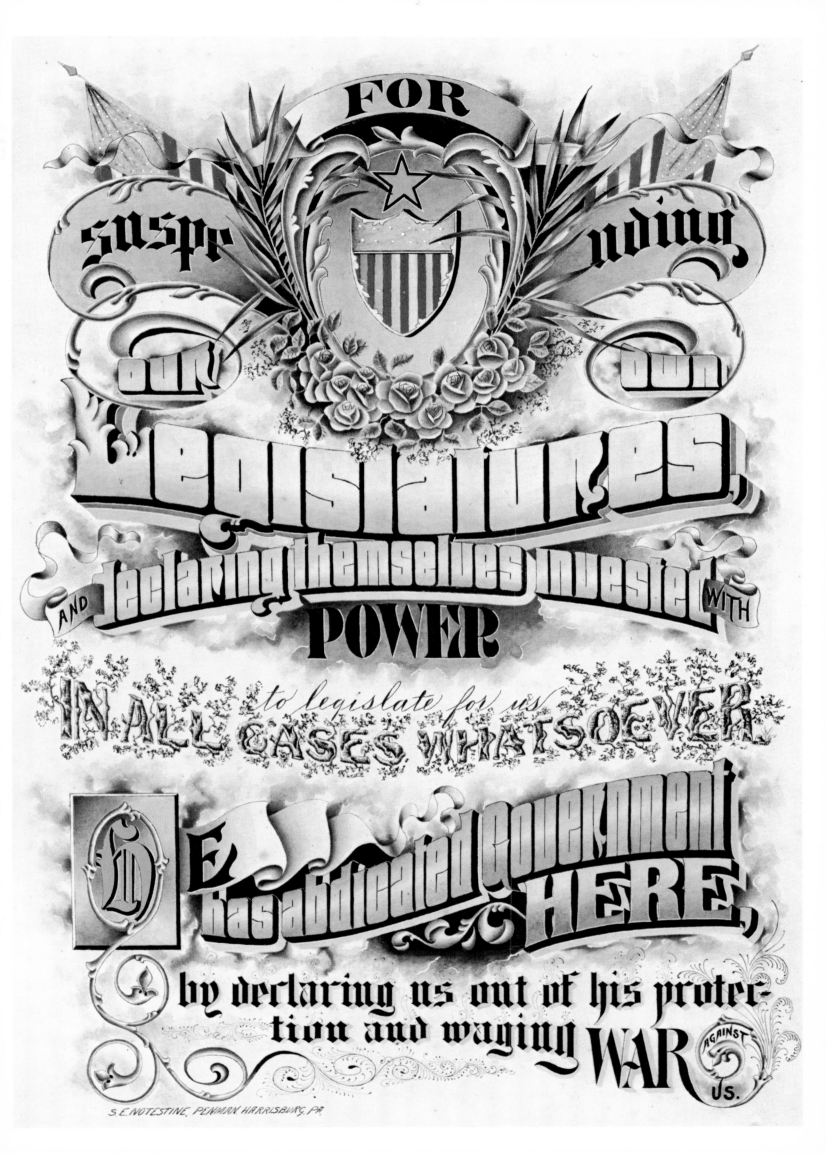

FOR suspending our own Legislatures, and declaring themselves invested with POWER to legislate for us IN ALL CASES WHATSOEVER.

HE has abdicated Government HERE, by declaring us out of his protection and waging WAR AGAINST US.

S.E. NOTESTINE, PENMAN, HARRISBURG, PA.

He has plundered our seas, ravaged our coasts, burnt our towns, and destroyed the lives of our people.

On September 21, 1776, a great fire swept British-held New York City and destroyed almost three hundred buildings. Detail from an engraving by Francis Xav. Habermann.

He is at this time transporting large armies of foreign mercenaries to compleat the works of death, desolation and tyranny already begun with circumstances of cruelty & perfidy scarcely paralleled in the most barbarous ages and totally unworthy the Head of a civilized nation.

Above: British and Hessian soldiers at the time of the War of Independence. *Below:* On December 26, 1776, the Hessian mercenary troops were put to flight when George Washington crossed the ice-choked Delaware River at night and attacked by surprise.

He has constrained our fellow Citizens taken Captive on the high Seas to bear arms against their country, to become the executioners of their friends and brethren, or to fall themselves by their hands.

American sailors in bondage in the hold of the *Trenton*.

It has constrained our fellow Citizens taken Captive ON THE HIGH SEAS to bear arms against their COUNTRY, to become the executioners of their friends AND BRETHREN, or to fall themselves BY THEIR Hands

He has excited domestic insurrection amongst us, and has endeavoured to bring on the inhabitants of our frontiers,*the merciless Indian Savages, whose known rule of warfare, is an undistinguished destruction of all ages, sexes and conditions.

*This comma, also found in the original copy of the Declaration, is an incorrect separation of subject and verb.

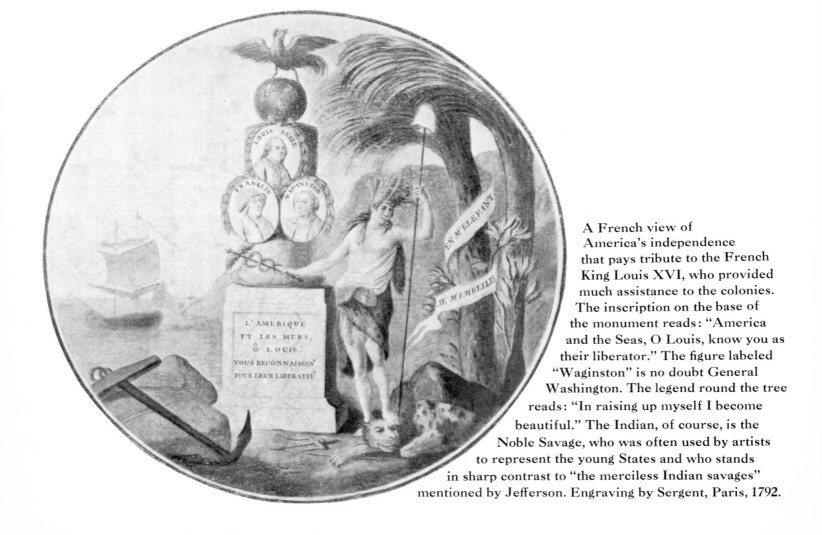

A French view of America's independence that pays tribute to the French King Louis XVI, who provided much assistance to the colonies. The inscription on the base of the monument reads: "America and the Seas, O Louis, know you as their liberator." The figure labeled "Waginston" is no doubt General Washington. The legend round the tree reads: "In raising up myself I become beautiful." The Indian, of course, is the Noble Savage, who was often used by artists to represent the young States and who stands in sharp contrast to "the merciless Indian savages" mentioned by Jefferson. Engraving by Sergent, Paris, 1792.

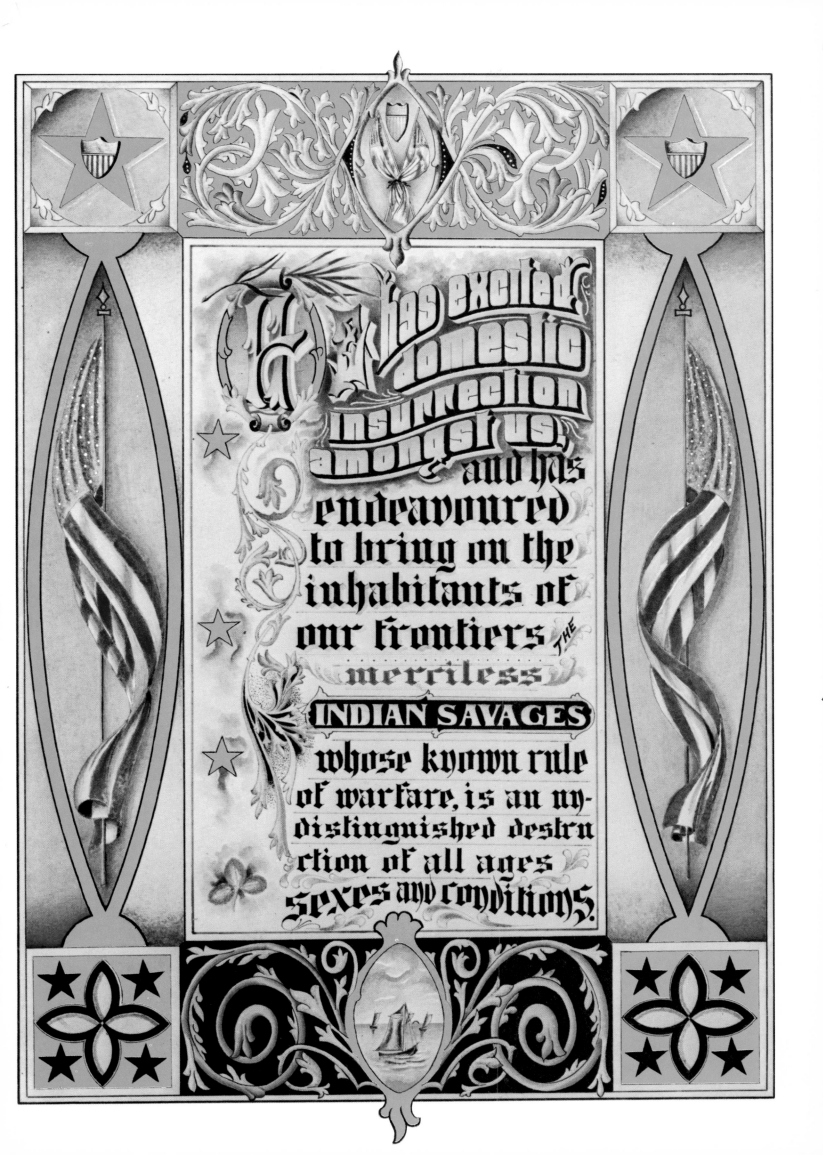

*In every stage of these Oppressions
we have Petitioned for Redress in the most humble terms:
Our repeated Petitions have been answered only by repea[t]
injury. A Prince, whose character is thus...*

Benjamin Franklin had been
sent to Britain to represent
the colonies at court. When
his mission failed he became
important in the drafting of
both the Declaration of
Independence and the
Constitution.

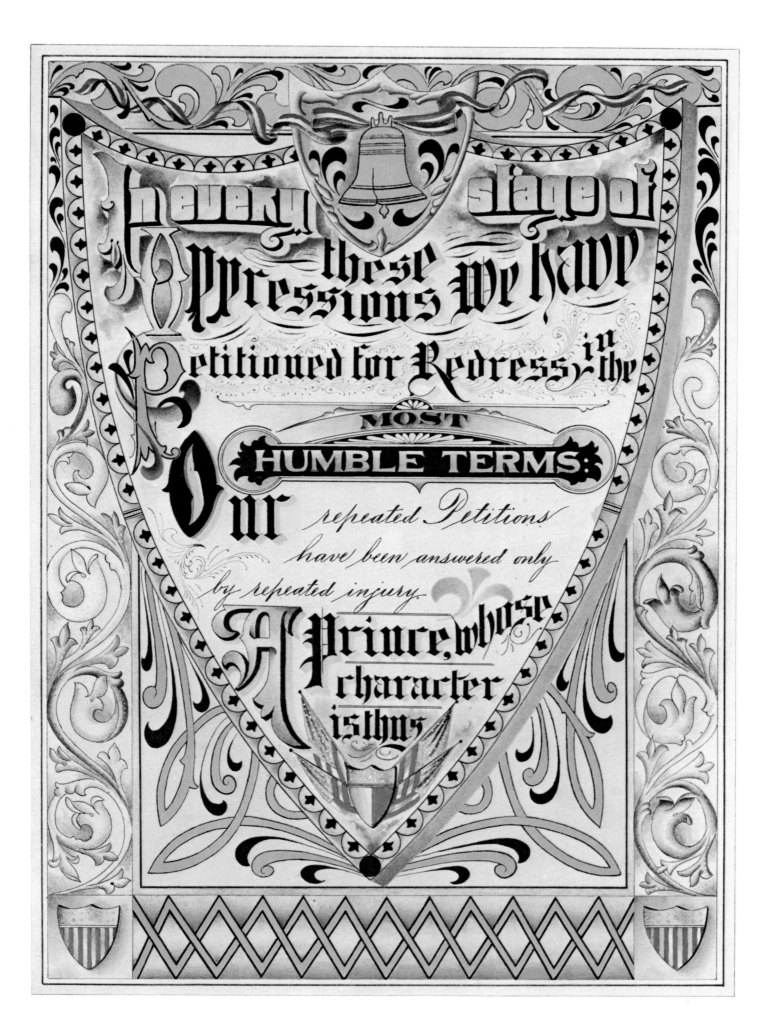

. . . marked by every art* which may define a Tyrant, is unfit to be the ruler of a free people. Nor have we been wanting in attention† to our . . .

*"Act" is correct.   †"Attentions" is correct.

Angry New Yorkers tearing down the statue of King George III in Bowling Green, 1776.

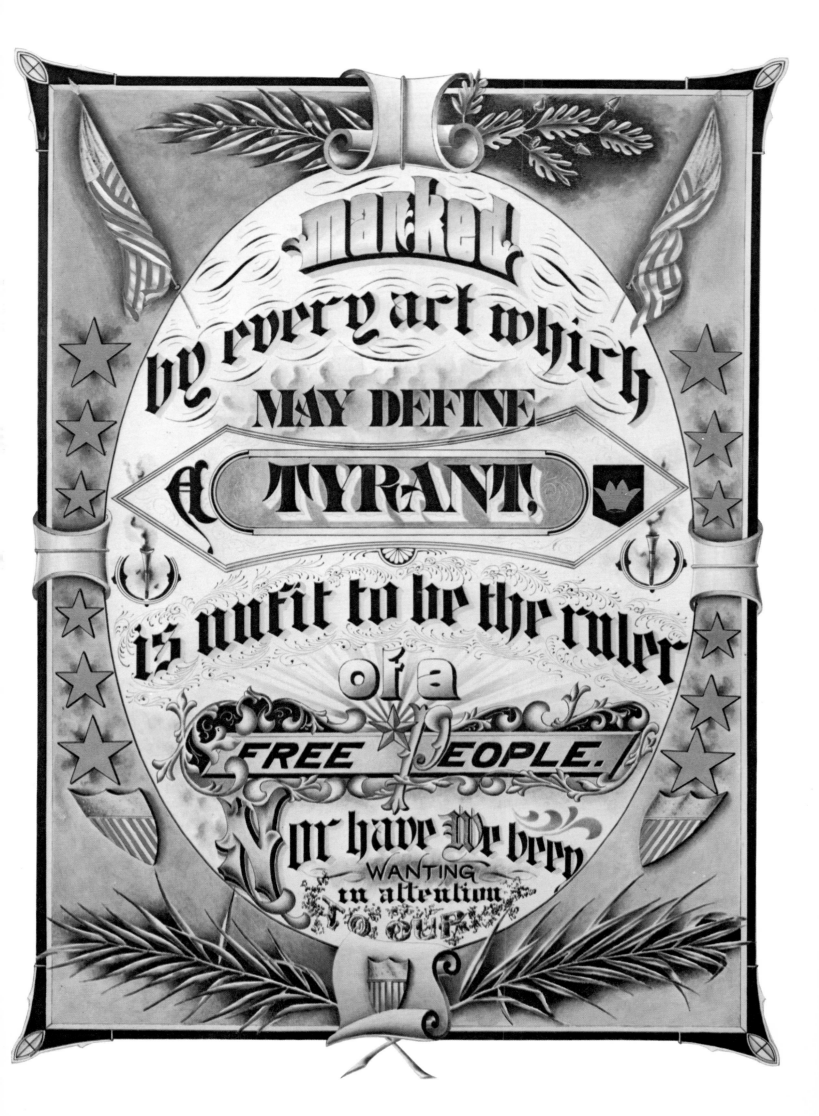

. . . British Brethren. We have warned them from time to time of attempts by their Legislature to extend an unwarrantable jurisdiction over us. We have reminded them of the . . .

The fourth page of Thomas Jefferson's original draft of the Declaration of Independence.

BRITISH BRETHREN.

WE

have warned them
from TIME OF ATTEMPTS time to
BY THEIR
Legislature
to
extend an
Unwarrantable jurisdic-
tion over us
WE have reminded them
OF THE

...circumstances of our emigration and settlement here. We have appealed to their native justice and magnanimity, and we have conjured them by the ties of our common kindred to disavow these usurpations, which,* would inevitably interrupt our connections and correspondence.

*Notestine mistakenly inserts a comma at this point.

Members of the First Continental Congress leaving Carpenter's Hall in Philadelphia, 1774. Painting from about 1910, by Clyde O. DeLong, a student of Howard Pyle's.

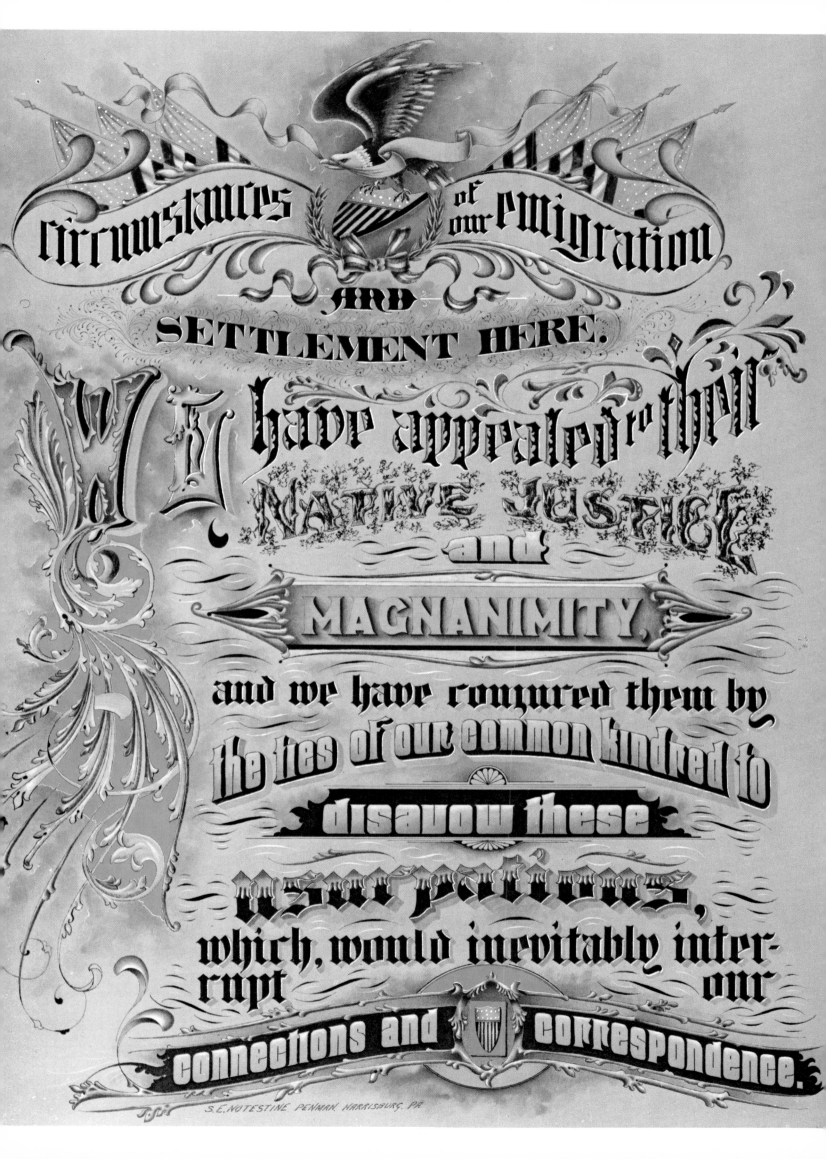

circumstances of our emigration

AND

SETTLEMENT HERE.

WE have appealed to their

NATIVE JUSTICE

and

MAGNANIMITY,

and we have conjured them by

the ties of our common kindred to

disavow these

usurpations,

which would inevitably interrupt our

connections and correspondence.

S.E. NOTESTINE PENMAN, HARRISBURG, PA

They too have been deaf to the voice of justice and of consanguinity. We must, therefore, acquiesce in the necessity which denounces our separation and hold them, as we hold the rest of mankind, Enemies in War, in Peace, Friends.

"Concord—the First Blow for Liberty" is the title of this engraving and refers to the battle between British troops and Minutemen that took place on April 19, 1775, in Massachusetts. It was the first effective demonstration of American power. Actually, the first military encounter took place on December 14, 1774, at Portsmouth, New Hampshire.

THEY too have been deaf TO THE VOICE OF JUSTICE and of consanguinity MUST, THEREFORE, ACQUIESCE in the necessity, which denounces OUR SEPARATION AND hold them, as we hold the rest of mankind, ENEMIES IN WAR, IN PEACE, FRIENDS

We, therefore, the Representatives of the United States of America, in General Congress assembled, appealing to the Supreme Judge of the world for the rectitude of our intentions, do, in the Name, and by the authority of the good People ...

John Binns marketed this ornamental engraving of the Declaration.

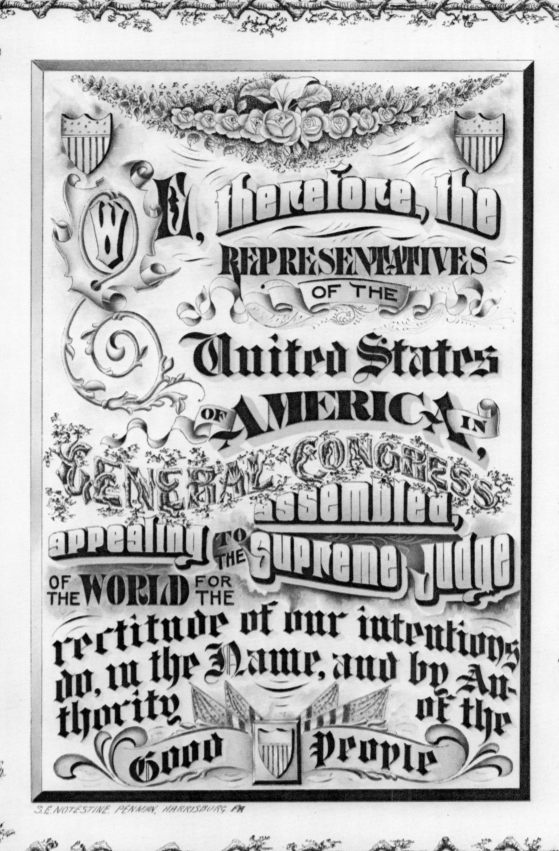

We, therefore, the REPRESENTATIVES OF THE United States of AMERICA, in GENERAL CONGRESS assembled, appealing to the Supreme Judge of the WORLD FOR THE rectitude of our intentions, do, in the Name, and by Authority of the Good People

S.E. NOTESTINE PENMAN, HARRISBURG PA

...of these Colonies, solemnly publish and declare, that these United Colonies are, and of Right ought to be, free and independent States; and* that they are absolved from all Allegiance to the British Crown ...

*No "and" in the original.

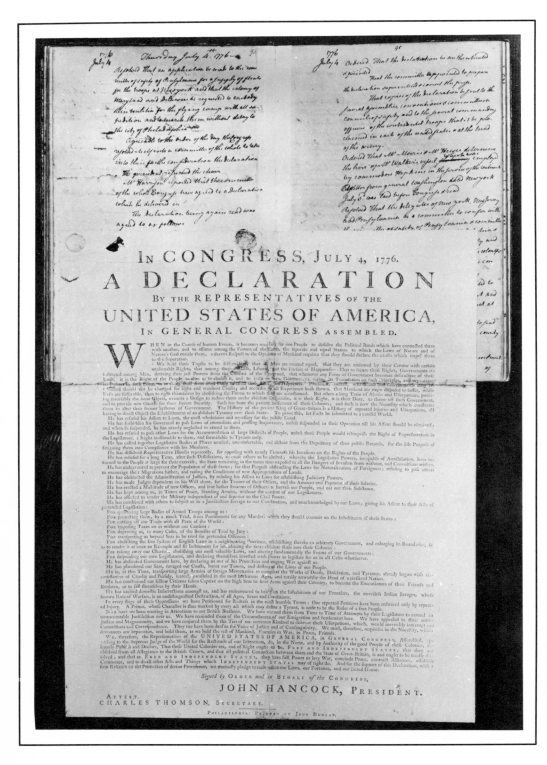

The actual Congressional Record for July 4, 1776, which records the adoption of the Declaration of Independence by the Second Continental Congress, with a printed copy of the Declaration that was pasted in the Record the next day, July 5.

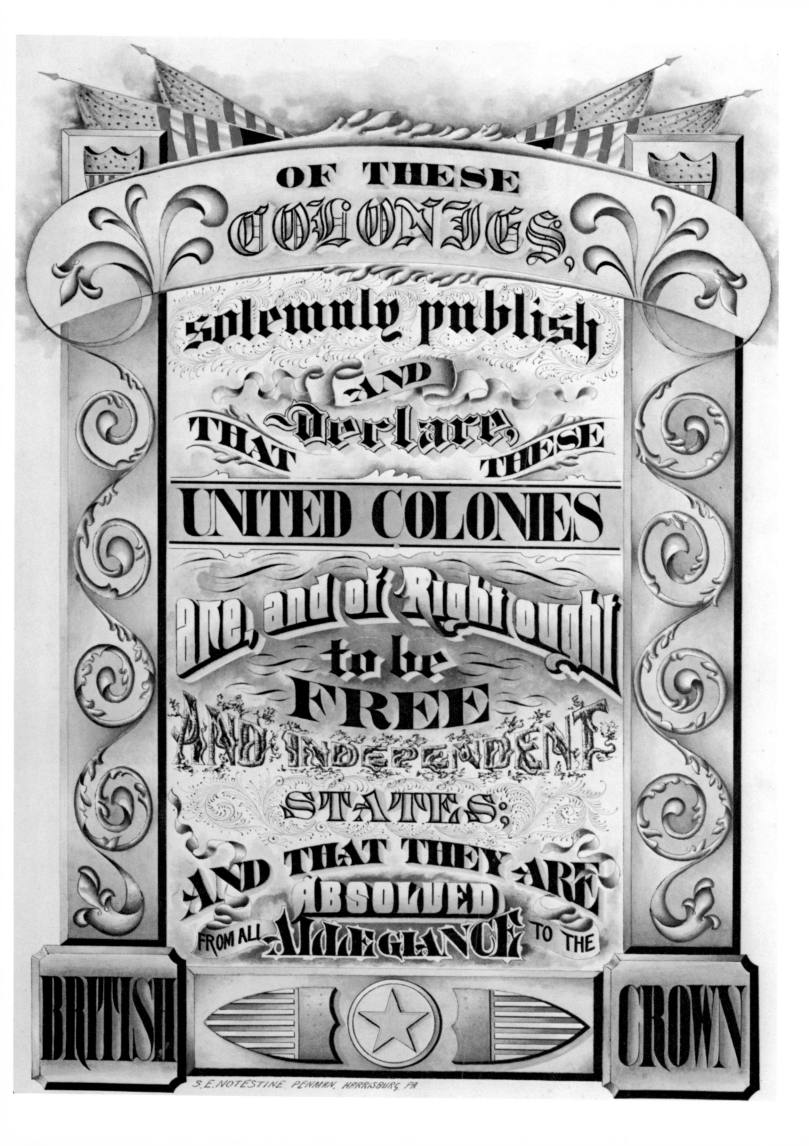

. . . and that all political connection between them and the State of Great Britain, is and ought to be totally dissolved; and that as Free and Independent States they have full Power to levy War, conclude Peace, contract Alliances, establish Commerce, and to do all other Acts and Things . . .

A British view of the United States in 1876. Uncle Sam appears to be a colorful talker whom John Bull, mopping his pate, has come to admire somewhat.

and that all political connection between them and THE State of Great Britain, is and ought to be TOTALLY DISSOLVED; and that as Free and Independent States they have full Power to levy WAR, conclude Peace, contract Alliances, establish Commerce, and to do all other Arts and Things

...which Independent States may of right do. And for the support of this Declaration, with a firm reliance on the protection of Divine Providence, we mutually pledge to each other our lives, our fortunes and our sacred honor.

About 1840, Edward Hicks, famous for "The Peaceable Kingdom," completed this painting of the signing of the Declaration of Independence.

The Centennial Fourth. Illumination of Madison Square, New York, July 4, 1876.